*a short guide to

WRITING A
CRITICAL REVIEW

REVISED EDITION

ELIOT D. ALLEN
Formerly Dean of Humanities
New York State University College
  of Arts and Sciences, Plattsburgh, New York

ETHEL B. COLBRUNN
Formerly Professor of English
Stetson University

everett/edwards, inc.
post office box 1060 / deland, florida 32720

Ninth Printing August 1978

Library of Congress Cataloging in Publication Data

Allen, Eliot D.

A short guide to writing a critical review.

1. Book reviewing. I. Colbrunn, Ethel B., joint author.
II. Title. III. Title: Writing a critical review.
PN98.B7A4 1976   808'.066'028   76-3586
ISBN 0-912112-20-4

Other Publications in this Series

The Student Writer's Guide, Revised 1976
Word Power: A Short Guide to Vocabulary and Spelling, Revised 1975
A Short Guide to Writing Better Themes, 1968
A Short Guide to Writing a Research Paper, Manuscript Form, and Documentation, Revised 1976
A Short Guide to Reading Imaginative Literature, 1975
A Short Guide to Independent Study and Research in Literature, 1975
General Semantics: Guide and Workbook, Revised 1974

TABLE OF CONTENTS

PREFACE

To the Teacher ...

One of the most common kinds of writing assignment in high school and college English is the review or "book report" on a literary work. We make our students read; then we expect them to write about what they have read. In preparing book reports, however, some students develop very bad critical principles or none whatsoever. Often the report is prescribed in a completely mechanical form: for example, author, title, summary of contents, mention of important characters or events, reader's reaction.

Such writing has two very unfortunate consequences. First, if the testimony of many students may be trusted, some do not read the book at all; they simply fill in the required information from the jacket, table of contents, or a random plunge into the text. The second consequence is perhaps even worse; though the student may actually read the book, the act of writing about it does not require or encourage any real understanding of its literary qualities, significance, or true meaning.

A good critical review, however, requires serious thought and personal involvement—the selection of aspects to discuss, the search for evidence to support opinions, and the judgment of ultimate appraisal. Through such an experience—and perhaps **only** through it—the student comes to understand and participate in the study of literature.

This booklet is intended primarily to help the student help himself. It may also be used more formally in class. The final section contains outlines of reviews. The works covered by these outlines may be assigned for outside reading and discussed in class. Then each student may be required to expand, with appropriate additions and insights, the outline given in the book, and finally, to write his own review based on that outline. This is an excellent preparatory step to completely independent writing. Or, if it is either inappropriate or inconvenient to assign these particular selections for reading, other works may be chosen and outlines prepared, with or without the class's help, patterned after the sample outlines. Of course, when the student progresses to preparing his outline independently, he may still refer to the sample as a model both for form and for content.

Many of the points under the sections "Preparing the Outline," "Writing the First Draft," and "Revising the Draft" are applicable to general composition work and can be used in teaching writing other than critical reviews.

The section entitled "Suggestions for Various Types of Reviews" is effective for classroom use as a basis for oral reviews. Assignments should include different kinds of poems, plays, and non-fictional works, as well as fiction; and class discussion or commentary by the teacher should emphasize the problems and possibilities of the various genres. This sort of oral review followed by informal analysis is especially valuable as a preliminary to writing reviews, as it reveals to the student some of the possibilities for diverse, original, and challenging approaches to writing a critical review.

E.D.A.
E.B.C.

iv

**WHAT IS A
CRITICAL REVIEW?** A critical review is a paper involving an opinion of, as well as some information about, a piece of writing, a play, or a program. It is **not a** summary of plot, a paraphrase, an outline, or a précis. It includes a statement of what the author or producer has tried to do, it evaluates how well (in the opinion of the reviewer) this person has succeeded, and it presents evidence to support this evaluation. Sufficient information should be given to allow the reader of the review to form his own opinion of the work in question.

The subjects which may be reviewed are varied. Most frequently a critical review deals with a literary work: a novel, novelette, short story, play, poem, or a piece of non-fiction prose, either book length or shorter, such as biography, history, or essay. Other subjects may include performances of a play either on the stage or on television, operas, operettas, radio and television programs, concerts, and exhibitions of paintings or sculpture.

**WHAT MUST THE
REVIEWER KNOW?** What must the reviewer know in order to write a critical review? The answer may be stated simply. He must know two things: the work he is reviewing and the requirements of the genre to which the work belongs. Knowing the work itself means no superficial, quick reading of the work but careful reading, usually at least twice. The reviewer must attempt to understand what the author or composer has had as a purpose and must try to perceive how each part of the work was meant to contribute. For example, in reviewing a drama the reviewer will consider how action, character, setting, and language work together and what part each plays in the whole.

A knowledge of the genre (that is, the type to which the work belongs, such as historical novel, lyric poem, classical tragedy, comic opera) is essential for a fair appraisal. For instance, to criticize a lyric poem because it lacks plot would be absurd. The greater the reviewer's knowledge of the type is, the more likely it is that the reviewer will be able to recognize variations within the type and to have a basis for judgment of the success of the particular work. To some extent, a comparison with other works of the same genre is inevitable although this comparison may not be expressed.

Narrowness of background may produce prejudices. As far as possible, it is the duty of the reviewer to be unbiased and completely fair to the author. This does not rule out, however, the right of the reviewer to express his opinion of the worthwhileness of the author's intentions. But his main business is to appraise the success or failure of the work judged by the seeming purpose of its creator. His skill as a reviewer will be shown largely by his choice of supporting evidence, but a reader will not respect the opinion of a reviewer who appears unfair to the author.

READING THE WORK

It would seem to be too obvious to require stating that the reviewer must begin by reading the work (or viewing the picture or hearing the opera) which he is to review. Yet many so-called "book reports" have been written on unread books.

First of all, the reading must be done carefully and thoroughly. Judgments based on hasty reading are almost inevitably unjust and are sometimes embarrassingly inaccurate. Read with a purpose: to discover the significant features of the book you are going to review. Significant for your review will be such matters as theme or purpose of the book, organization, style, particular virtues, and particular faults. From an appraisal of all these things must come your final judgment as to the aesthetic success or failure of the work.

Give your reading every opportunity to be thorough and perceptive by starting with as much information as possible. Look at the title, and at the subtitle if there is one. A glance at the table of contents (if it is that kind of a book) may orient you as to the general plan and let you see the organization in advance. A preface or introduction may well contain the clearest statement of the book's purpose, meaning, intention, scope, and limitations—only a foolish reviewer would overlook such material. It is important that you know what the writer was attempting to do and not condemn him for failure to do something that was not part of his purpose.

As you read, take notes on items that will be useful to your review. The opening part of the work is likely to be especially important. Note very brilliant passages or obvious flaws or weaknesses. You will probably need quotations or references to show what the theme of the work is; passages to illustrate style; examples of the author's technique in particular aspects, such as dialogue or description. The ending of a work is likely to be very significant.

We have just referred to the theme of the work. In most works of fiction, drama, or poetry, you will probably want to pay particular attention to the ways in which other aspects of the work, such as style or characterization, support and develop the theme. This matter is discussed briefly under the special suggestions for reviewing the short story, on p. 11.

Probably your notes will be most efficient and useful if they consist of references to particular passages of the book, along with your own brief comment as to what use you might make of them in your review.

BACKGROUND FOR REVIEWING

Whatever the work is which you are reviewing, it is an example of a particular art form—e.g., the novel, the short story, the play, the opera, the symphony, the sonata, the portrait, the landscape, the abstraction. You cannot expect to think clearly or write well about the work if you do not know at least something about the art form and how it functions. There are probably at least a few critical terms useful in the discussion of the art that you will need to know and be able to use if your review is to seem knowledgeable and finished.

It is likely that you may already have studied enough about the art form with which you are working so that you are ready to write a review. If not, you need some background. There are many, many works which will give you an acquaintance with the fundamentals you need. Here are a few suggestions in various fields:

Poetry

Perrine, Laurence. *Sound and Sense: An Introduction to Poetry.* 2nd ed. New York: Harcourt, Brace and World, 1963.

Ribner, Irving, and Harry Morris. *Poetry: A Critical and Historical Introduction.* Chicago: Scott, Foresman, 1962.

Schneider, Elisabeth. *Poems and Poetry.* New York: American Book Company, 1964.

Drama

Altenbernd, Lynn, and Leslie Lewis. *Introduction to Literature: Plays.* New York: Macmillan, 1963.

Bierman, Judith, James Hart, and Stanley Johnson. *The Dramatic Experience.* Englewood Cliffs, N. J.: Prentice-Hall, 1958.

Kernan, Alvin. *Character and Conflict: An Introduction to Drama.* New York: Harcourt, Brace and World, 1963.

Fiction

Brooks, Cleanth, and Robert Penn Warren. *Understanding Fiction.* 2nd ed. New York: Appleton, Century, Crofts, 1959.

Perrine, Laurence. *Story and Structure.* New York: Harcourt, Brace and World, 1959.

Thurston, Jarvis A. *Reading Modern Short Stories.* Chicago: Scott, Foresman, 1955.

Biography
>Johnson, Edgar. *One Mighty Torrent*. New York: Macmillan, 1955. Introduction and Chapter 1.

Music
>Miller, Hugh. *Introduction to Music*. New York: Barnes and Noble, 1959.

>_____. *History of Music*. New York: Barnes and Noble, 1958.

Painting and Sculpture
>Janson, H. W. *History of Art*. New York: Abrams, 1962.
>Lowry, Bates. *The Visual Experience*. Englewood Cliffs, N. J.: Prentice-Hall, 1961.

General Criticism
>Crane, R. S., ed. *Critics and Criticism*. Chicago: University of Chicago Press, 1952.
>Gardner, Helen. *The Business of Criticism*. New York: Oxford University Press, 1963.

ABOUT THE AUTHOR/ARTIST

The reviewer should tell his readers something about the artist who has created the work he is reviewing. "Something" does not mean a biography, or a hodge-podge of whatever facts the reviewer can glean from *Who's Who* or the *World Almanac*. But to understand a work of art, we often are helped by a knowledge of the writer's nationality, of the period in which he lived, and of any particular political, social, philosophic, or aesthetic movements with which he was associated.

Such information may be only a sentence or two; in a longer review, it may occupy several paragraphs. The important thing is that the information given be relevant to the subject of the review, and that it contribute to the main and only justifiable purpose of the whole review itself: to help the reader understand and evaluate the work under discussion.

**PREPARING
THE OUTLINE**

Always make an outline before you write a review. Only by doing so can you hope to get an over-all grasp of the organization of your paper. The outline stage is the most efficient time to rearrange material, eliminate irrelevant items, and discover gaps and weaknesses in your coverage. An hour spent in outlining and carefully arranging your material may save you several hours of writing time and produce a better finished product as well.

Before starting your outline you should decide what your thesis will be. There should be a central point in your review around which all points will be made. So begin by asking yourself what main point or idea you wish to make. Write this down as your thesis, and later check all parts of the outline against this to see whether each part defines, explains, supports, develops, or otherwise contributes to the thesis.

Now go over the notes you have made and eliminate any which seem to have no relationship to your thesis. Next group together the notes which deal with specific aspects of your subject. You will probably have several groups: for example, notes on the characters, notes on the setting, or other aspects. Next decide in which order the topics should be treated for the most effective presentation, keeping in mind that clarity, coherence, and emphasis may be affected by the arrangement of the divisions in your review. Do not let the number of notes you have for each topic determine the importance you should give to the topic. It may be necessary to select only part of the material at hand for one division and to go back to the work being reviewed for further support of another division.

Write down all the major headings of the outline first; then fill in the subdivisions. Check each item to see whether it logically belongs under its heading. Ask yourself whether you are stressing the most important things and whether this is the best possible arrangement of parts. Check the relevance of each part to the thesis.

**WRITING THE
FIRST DRAFT**

Keep before you your thesis statement and outline. Remember that a critical review is a statement of opinion but must be the considered judgment of the writer after he has determined the author's purpose. You should state what you believe to be the author's purpose and how well you think he has achieved his purpose; then give evidence to support your judgment. If, in your opinion, the purpose is an unworthy one, you have the privilege of saying so; but, in fairness, if the author succeeds in doing what he set out to do, you should say that.

For your convenience in revising, be sure to leave wide margins and double or triple-space if typing, or to write on every other line if writing by hand. A good rough draft has room for corrections.

There are several ways you may begin. You may start by stating your thesis; by stating the author's purpose; by stating the problem treated by the book (whether social, philosophical, psychological, or otherwise); by telling the author's qualifications; by classifying the work within the type or genre to which it belongs; by presenting historical background for the work; or by pointing out the significance of the work for our generation or time. If the reader is likely to be unfamiliar with the work, it is permissible to begin by summarizing briefly the content (this does not mean a plot summary in the case of a novel, short story, or play). Remember that the opening paragraph is a position of emphasis, often sets the tone of the paper, and may determine the reader's response to the paper as a whole. You want to capture the reader's interest, but be careful not to make such a bold statement that you are forced to contradict yourself later.

If you have prepared your outline carefully, you should be able to follow it point by point after your introductory paragraph. You may find that you need to make changes in the outline. You will perhaps need to add transitional paragraphs between major divisions. A transitional sentence at the end of one paragraph or the beginning of the next may be sufficient. Aim at smoothness and logical development. Be sure that the supporting evidence you give is clearly related to the point you are making. Be careful to place within quotation marks or indent and set off any quoted material. This will make your rewriting easier.

The concluding paragraph may be a summing up or a restating of your thesis. If you have made several points, it may be helpful to summarize these. You may save your final judgment of the work as a whole for the conclusion. But do not add a new idea which you leave undeveloped. The beginning and end of the review are the two most emphatic parts.

REVISING THE DRAFT

There is no point in making a rough draft of a piece of composition unless you revise it before making the final copy. If you are not going to revise, you might just as well make the final copy to begin with, and submit it, mistakes and all.

Here are some steps to help you in revision:

1. **When you have finished your draft, allow some time, preferably at least a day, to elapse before you start revision.** During this time your mind has a chance to forget what you said or intended to say; when you reread your draft, you can see it as it is, with a certain amount of objectivity.

2. **Read your draft out loud at least once.** The ear can often detect slips or infelicities which the eye may pass over. Furthermore, reading out loud will help you to read slowly enough so that you can pay attention to what you have written.

3. Correct all errors of mechanics—spelling, grammar, punctuation—at once as you find them. **Do not let a mistake go unmarked and plan to correct it in the final copy.** This is one way mistakes get into the final copy.

4. **Read through again looking particularly for unity and organization.** Consult your outline again and have clearly in mind what you wanted to say. Have you said it? Have you excluded extraneous material? Have you arranged your material in the best possible order? Do your illustrations—quoted passages, and so on, if you have used them— really illustrate what they are intended to illustrate?

5. **Do not hesitate to make major revisions in your draft,** if necessary, by cutting up your pages to rearrange paragraphs or to make insertions. Often a convenient way to add material is to divide the page at the point where the material is to be put in, type or write the new material, and staple the pieces of paper back together again in the correct order. An unsightly rough draft, when you have finished with it, is often a sign of a potentially good composition.

6. **Verify any quotations for accuracy** and be sure that all your sources are properly and clearly indicated. Do not leave this process to the final draft, where you may omit a source reference or give the wrong one.

7. **Your rough draft is finished only when you are ready to make your final copy from it** word for word as you have finally revised it. If much revision was necessary, you may have to make a second draft in order to get a clear enough copy to correct for your final draft. Some writers make many, many drafts before they are satisfied with the final product.

8. When you are ready to make your final copy, be sure that you have an adequate supply of uniform paper of the prescribed kind; that your typewriter ribbon is good (if you are typing), or that you will not have to change ink color in the middle (if you are writing it by hand).

Copy carefully. If you are a poor speller, have a dictionary handy to verify the spelling of any word of which you are even slightly doubtful.

9. When you have finished your final copy, put it aside for a while before you go over it for your last reading. Immediate rereading often lets your mind assume that what you intended to write is what is actually on the paper; if you can wait for a while until you have forgotten what you wrote, you will have to read it word for word, and thus may see typographical or other errors. One good plan is to move a sheet of paper down the page slowly as you read, allowing your eye to concentrate on only one line at a time.

10. If corrections are necessary, make neat erasures or additions. Use a caret (like this ʌ) to mark insertions. If ink corrections are necessary on a typed page, try to use an ink of the same color as your typing. **Do not hesitate to recopy a page which contains many errors.** If you have your paper typed by someone else, do not trust the final rereading to him: it is up to you to be sure that your final copy is correct and accurate.

DOCUMENTATION

If your review is of a book, short story, poem, or the printed version of a play, you should indicate author, title, place of publication, publisher, and date of publication either in a subtitle or else in a footnote at or near the beginning of your review. Passages quoted from the work should also be footnoted, as should be references to particular passages if the reader must be able to identify them in order to understand what you have said about them.

In a critical review you are likely to use footnotes, other than those already referred to, as a means of acknowledging other sources, such as other reviews, criticisms, or biographies which you may have used. Direct quotations should always be footnoted. Ideas borrowed from another writer, whether quoted verbatim or not, should also be acknowledged. Paraphrasing another writer does **not** remove the need for acknowledgement (and is often a form of plagiarism, whether acknowledged or not).

To make a footnote, place a reference number (²) in the text after the matter to be documented, half a line above the line of the text. Place a corresponding number before, and above, the footnote on a separate page at the end of your review.

Indent each footnote as you would a paragraph. Double space. Number footnotes consecutively throughout the paper. Examples of footnotes and bibliography in correct form are to be found in the sample critical review, pp. 20-26.

For a fuller discussion of footnoting and manuscript form, as well as a simple explanation of plagiarism and how to avoid it, see Eliot D. Allen and Ethel B. Colbrunn, *A Short Guide to Writing a Research Paper, Manuscript Form, and Documentation* (Deland, Florida: everett/edwards, inc., Newly Revised Edition, 1976).

WHAT NOT TO DO

DO NOT write a review of a book you have not read, a performance of a play you have not seen, or a piece of music you have not heard. Honest reviewing begins with an honest acquaintance with the work to be reviewed.

DO NOT summarize the work or write a précis or paraphrase. A critical review is not a report or summary. A brief summary of what the work covers may be justified but should never be the major portion.

DO NOT write a character analysis or otherwise limit the review to only one aspect of the work.

DO NOT spend as much or more space on the biography of, and other works by, the author as upon the work under consideration. You are judging the work, not the man or his other work.

DO NOT allow prejudice to make you unfair. You may disagree with the author's viewpoint without disapproving of the work. In other words, the critic must be able to detach himself from the work although he may give his impression of it.

DO NOT give others' opinions without telling whether you agree or disagree with them. **You** are the critic. You may read about the author or work for helping your understanding of it, but the critical review should be your personal judgment.

DO NOT indulge your own wit and brilliance at the expense of a true appraisal of the work you are reviewing. Never distort the facts or misinterpret the ideas for the sake of a chance to show off as a critic. A good review is an honest and fair one.

SUGGESTIONS FOR VARIOUS TYPES OF REVIEW

The instructions above are designed to help you with the general problem of writing a critical review. Your particular problem will depend on what kind of a work you are reviewing. In the sections which follow, you will find suggestions about reviewing various sorts of works.

THE NOVEL

Novels are likely to be long and complex. The inexperienced reviewer may think that the best thing he can do is to summarize the story. Generally speaking, this is the worst thing he can do. A critical review of a novel is **not** a retelling of the plot of the novel. An attempt at summary in any detail at all may leave you with a long, involved—and generally confusing—narrative that takes up more space than you had intended for the whole review—and your review is still unwritten.

It is perfectly appropriate, however, for the review to tell something about the nature of the story. To say that *The Heart of Midlothian* by Sir Walter Scott "is a historical novel set in eighteenth-century Scotland and England" tells the reader what sort of novel it is without involving the reviewer in a summary of the plot. It would not be summarizing the plot to describe F. Scott Fitzgerald's *Tender Is the Night* as "the story of an American psychiatrist and his wife and friends set in post-World War I Europe."

Since the beginnings of long narrative fiction in English, readers have been especially interested in character portrayal. No reviewer of a novel can afford to omit critical attention to the types of characters present, the author's technique in revealing them, and their appeal and convincingness to the reader. Thus, in reviewing Hardy's *The Mayor of Casterbridge,* you might well point out how Hardy deliberately develops parallels and contrasts between the two leading male characters and also between the two leading female characters. You might also go on to point out which of these characters is most effective in conveying to the reader what Hardy has to say about life.

Every novel has a setting, but setting is not of equal importance in every novel. Where it is especially important, you should discuss its role in the novel. For example, in Hardy's *The Return of the Native,* the setting is at least as important as any one of the characters. In many historical novels, the setting and the author's treatment of it will deserve space in a good review.

Especially since the middle of the nineteenth century, the novel has often been used as a vehicle for propaganda or at least for the author's political, social, or philosophical ideas. When such a purpose is present, you should certainly point it out. To review Dickens' *Nicholas Nickleby* without mentioning the ferocious indictment Dickens makes of private schools would be to miss an important element in the novel. Of course as a reviewer, you are not bound to the same views as the author. In reviewing Steinbeck's *The Grapes of Wrath,* for example, you ought surely to call attention to Steinbeck's emotional outcry against economic injustice; whether you question the validity of the case Steinbeck tries to make will depend on your own views.

Whether or not the novel contains actual propaganda, most serious novels have a theme. As a reviewer, you should attempt to determine what the theme is, how valid or significant it is, and how well the author has developed and supported it. Other elements which may be present in the novel you are reviewing, and which, therefore, may need to be discussed in your review, are symbolism, satire, and irony.

THE SHORT STORY   The modern short story, as an art form, is expected to be highly unified and to make some kind of significant revelation to the reader: Older short stories, as well as most of those written purely for entertainment, are likely to settle, instead, for simply an interesting narrative.

As with the novel, the reviewer of the short story should avoid a summary of the plot. Discussion of characters is most appropriate; setting, if important, should be considered. Short stories written during the last half century as serious, interpretive literature almost invariably have a central theme to which all elements in the story contribute. The perceptive reviewer should probably make the main part of his critical review of such a short story a discussion of this theme, the method by which it is revealed, and its significance for the reader.

In the well-unified short story, theme will usually be inseparable, finally, from the other elements in the story. This fusion may present a problem in organization, since a discussion of one element leads you at once into others. In such a story as Joseph Conrad's **The Secret Sharer,** for instance, the harmony of plot, character, symbolism, and theme is nearly perfect; and as a perceptive reviewer, you will see the fusion of these elements not as an obstacle to your review, but as a mark of distinction in the art of the writer.

THE BIOGRAPHY   Presumably a biography seeks first of all to give an accurate representation of the life of the person about whom it is written. Ideally, therefore, to review a biography, you should yourself be so well informed about the subject that you can discuss the accuracy of the representation with some authority. Student writers of critical reviews are, however, not likely to be in this fortunate position, and so must often turn to other aspects of the work. If you are able to choose among a number of biographies to review, you would do well to choose one where your previous knowledge of, or interest in, the subject or period gives you a head start.

If there is any great crux, problem, or mystery in the life of the subject of the biography, you will surely want to discuss whatever treatment the biographer has made of this matter, for it may be one of the distinguishing features of the particular biography. Anyone reviewing, for example, a biography of Ambrose Bierce would probably want to mention the biographer's theory as to the time and place of Bierce's death.

Most biography, in addition to reporting dates, events, names, and places, and so forth, seeks to interpret its subject to the reader. An important consideration for you, therefore, will be to determine what interpretation the biographer has given, how it differs from previous interpretations perhaps, and how convincing and satisfying, as an aid to understanding the personality of the subject, this interpretation is.

Another common, useful, and legitimate aim of the biographer is to give a picture of the life and times in which his subject lived— *e.g.,* Carl Sandburg's *Abraham Lincoln: The War Years,* a four-volume work which gives vivid insights into the U.S. of the Civil War period. A reviewer would certainly want to discuss the success of this aspect of the biographer's art.

OTHER NON-FICTION PROSE

Other non-fiction prose may generally be classified under four kinds: (1) the informal essay or personal reminiscences, (2) the persuasive argument, (3) informational expository prose, and (4) criticism. The first type is usually meant to entertain, but the other three types serve other specific purposes, and determination of the author's purpose is particularly important in reviewing any of these. Let us consider each type separately.

The **informal essay** or book of reminiscences depends greatly upon the style of the author for its success. Consequently, you need to consider the quality of the prose and the tone: solemn, humorous, whimsical, nostalgic, or whatever it may be. The personality of the author frequently gives a special flavor to the style which makes it distinctive. If so, you should discuss this as well as the thesis or central idea. If the book or essay is by or about a famous person, the interest is heightened. You need to distinguish between the interest due to the matter, and pleasure due to an interesting style. A book may be popular because of its subject without being a well-written book. Sometimes it is advisable for a reviewer to specify the kind of reader who will enjoy the work .

The **persuasive argument** should have a thesis either stated or implied. You judge the argument on how well the thesis is developed and proved. How true are the basic assumptions? how logical are the steps in the argument? how reliable is the conclusion? You will also consider the bias of the writer and what his motives are. Does he present both sides of the case and answer the opposition or does he show only his own side? (Are you letting your own bias determine your reaction, or are you remaining detached and as fair as possible?) What are the qualifications of the author for writing on the subject? Is he a recognized authority? Does he use propaganda devices such as glittering generalities, band-wagon, or stacking the cards? Who is his reading public and how effective is his work for his particular intended audience? How limited is this audience? You may not want or need to answer all of these questions in your review, but if you ask yourself the questions, it will probably help you to understand the writing and its purpose.

Informational prose may be varied in form and content but will have a common feature: its purpose is to give information. Included are scientific writing, histories, and factual reports of any kind. Of special importance for consideration of informational prose are three things: the authority of the author (how well qualified he is on the subject), the date of writing (since research may bring new light which makes an old work out-of-date), and the restrictions or limitations of the work. You should mention the style, clarity of exposition, and the difficulty of the vocabulary and point out whether the work is of a popular or scholarly nature. Expository prose may be written in a distinguished style which makes it a work of literary value. This is particularly true of histories, and consequently some older historians continue to be read as literature. Make a distinction, therefore, between the work valued for its style and the work valued solely for the information it gives. Ask how accurate and how complete the information is. Is the report of real significance? Is it of interest to a limited group only or to the general public?

You may be asked to write a **critical review** of a published critical work. Find out about the author and his reputation as a critic. How well qualified is he to write on the subject? Be sure to state his thesis and pass judgment on how well he has supported it. In judging criticism you can partly apply the instructions given in this booklet on writing a critical review; but remember that a long critical work may have another purpose than yours. Note what limitations the author has set for himself. If it is a scholarly work do not criticize the author for aiming his style towards a scholarly audience. Criticism involves opinions, so you may well ask some of the questions suggested for judging an argument; but most critical writing is not intended to persuade, and the good critic generally tries to maintain emotional detachment rather than involvement.

THE POEM

Since the length of a poem may vary from two lines to several hundred pages and since there are various types of poetry, you will do well to classify the poem you are reviewing unless it is so well known that all readers of your review are familiar with the poem. Such an identification also saves the reviewer from certain descriptions. For example, if you say that a poem is an Italian sonnet, you do not need to mention the number of lines, the foot, or meter, or rime scheme. The lyric, ballad, epic, dramatic monologue, and elegy all imply certain qualities or characteristics. You may want to state that the poem is regular or to point out the ways in which it varies from the usual poem in its genre.

A poem should be judged by the organic whole and by the unity of the parts. One looks for sincerity and originality of expression, but a poem also has form. Note the verse form and stanza pattern, the tone, and any poetic devices which affect the total impression. If the imagery is conspicuous for amount or originality, discuss it. Do likewise with sound devices (such as alliteration, assonance, onomatopoeia), but only if the poet seems to be using them for a purpose.

The meaning of a poem is important, but remember that what the poem says is not so important as how it says it. Do not write a paraphrase. Instead, try stating the theme. Ask yourself how the imagery, vocabulary, rhythm, form, and other aspects fit the theme and contribute to or take from the effectiveness of the poem as a whole, as a unit.

Use carefully selected passages from the poem to illustrate points and to support your opinions.

What has been said above pertains to a review of one poem, short or long. You may write a review of a collection of poems. If they are all by one poet you may discuss the poet's characteristics in general, his distinctive style or theme, or his varied styles and themes. You may choose to select one poem as representative and discuss it in more detail. If, on the other hand, the collection contains poems by several authors, discuss the editor's purpose in bringing together the group of poems and judge the editor's choice. Again you may wish to select one poem as representative or you may wish to emphasize the variety by discussing several poems.

THE PLAY, TELEVISION PLAY, OR MOVIE

Whether the play being reviewed is read or seen, it is well to state the type to which it belongs: tragedy, comedy, farce, fantasy, and also the treatment: realistic, naturalistic, or expressionistic. If the play is a Greek drama or in the style of Greek drama; if in the neoclassic style observing strictly the unities of time, place, and action; if a morality play in which the characters are personifications of abstract qualities; or if any other particular style is used, comment on this.

With all kinds of plays, as with all other kinds of writing, the first task of the reviewer is to determine the author's purpose. This means to decide not only whether the author intended solely to entertain or to present a thesis, to teach, or to persuade but also whether he was most interested in setting, in characterization, in plot, or in meaning.

In analyzing the play, consider the setting, action (or plot), characters, language, and meaning. If the play is successful all parts should work together to create a unified impression, and the first four elements should all contribute to the meaning. In discussing action consider the exposition, rising action, climax, and falling action. All drama involves conflict; what is the nature of the conflict or conflicts in this play? Are the characters individuals or types? Static or developing? Does the author present a view of life, or is his purpose to entertain, or both?

If you are reviewing a play you have seen performed, include an evaluation of the direction and the actors' performances. The setting, costumes, lighting and sound effects may be commented upon for attractiveness as well as for effectiveness in contributing to the meaning of the play.

Any playwright is likely to have a particular type of audience in mind, but this is especially true for radio plays, television plays, and movies. Try to determine which type of audience the play in question was meant for or is likely to please. Notice whether the plot has been manipulated or the ending contrived to produce an unlikely happy ending. Has the artistic unity been destroyed?

If the television play or movie is an adaptation of a stage play, short story, or novel, special comment on the changes made and skill of the adapter may be in order. If the play is based on history, its truth to historical facts and to the portrayal of historical characters needs to be evaluated.

SAMPLE OUTLINE (NOVEL)

Title: Ernest Hemingway's <u>The Old Man and the Sea</u>:

Dignity in Defeat

Thesis: The novel gives Hemingway's clearest statement

of the plight of man in a hostile environment.

I. Relationship to Hemingway's other work

   A. Settings reflect Hemingway's experiences

   1. Italy in World War I: <u>A Farewell to Arms</u>

   2. Life on continent: <u>The Sun Also Rises</u>

   3. Spanish Civil War: <u>For Whom the Bell Tolls</u>

   4. Retirement to Cuba: <u>The Old Man and the Sea</u>

   B. Subjects reflect Hemingway's interests

   1. Medical service: <u>A Farewell to Arms</u>

   2. Bullfighting: <u>The Sun Also Rises</u>

   3. The Spanish Loyalist cause: <u>For Whom the Bell Tolls</u>

   4. The Cuban people and deep sea fishing: <u>The Old Man and the Sea</u>

II. Style

   A. The familiar short clipped Hemingway prose

   B. The use of dialogue or interior monologue to carry the action

   C. Simple language expressing timeless truths

III. Character

   A. Only two characters as individuals of any consequence

   B. The boy

   C. Santiago

   1. A Simple, uneducated fisherman

      2.   A wise and dignified old man

      3.   An unbroken spirit in an exhausted body

IV. Theme

    A.   Hemingway's view of the plight of man in a hostile environment against which he must struggle although it will defeat him

      1.   Familiar echoes of same theme in his previous novels

      2.   A clearer statement in The Old Man and the Sea since it is removed from the confusions of war, politics, and love

    B.   Levels of interpretation seen by the critics

    C.   The universality of the theme

Ernest Hemingway's The Old Man and

the Sea: Dignity in Defeat

by Edith Dodd

English 202, Section 3

Professor Block

May 1, 1975

The Old Man and the Sea[1] is Ernest Hemingway's last novel. Published in 1952, the year Hemingway received the Nobel Prize for literature, it is a fitting and appropriate capstone to Hemingway's major works of fiction. It very clearly belongs to the family of Hemingway novels--works which invariably follow their author in his wanderings about the world. In 1918 Hemingway went to Italy and Switzerland; this is the setting of A Farewell to Arms. In the 1920's he lived chiefly in Europe; The Sun Also Rises is set in France and Spain. In 1937 Hemingway went to Spain as a war correspondent; the result was For Whom the Bell Tolls. And so it is not surprising that after Hemingway's long residence in Cuba, The Old Man and the Sea should have a Cuban setting.

Like his location of the moment, Hemingway's interests and activities are reflected in his novels. The army medical service appears in A Farewell to Arms; bullfighting plays an important part in The Sun Also Rises; the experiences and knowledge which came to Hemingway as war correspondent have their place in For Whom the Bell Tolls. The same is true for The Old Man and the Sea. Hemingway had long been fond of deep sea fishing, and his years in Cuba made him an avid follower of the sport.

If The Old Man and the Sea had for some reason appeared anonymously, few educated readers would have had trouble identifying its author. The terse, controlled prose bears the Hemingway hallmark, whether it describes a man: "The old man was thin and gaunt with deep wrinkles in the back of his neck. The brown blotches of the benevolent skin cancer the sun brings from its reflections on the tropic sea were on his cheeks.

The blotches ran well down the sides of his face and his hands had the deep-creased scars from handling heavy fish on the cords" (pp. 9-10) or looks at the sky and the sea: "The clouds over the land now rose like mountains and the coast was only a long green line with the gray blue hills behind it. The water was a dark blue now, so dark it was almost purple. As he looked down into it he saw the red sifting of the plankton in the dark water and the strange light the sun now made" (p. 38).

Because most of the action of this novel takes place while the main character is alone in a small boat, dialogue does not play as large a part as in Hemingway's earlier novels. But still there is the famous Hemingway conversation, for the old man thinks either to himself or out loud a great deal: "'Fish,' the old man said, 'Fish, you are going to have to die anyway. Do you have to kill me too?'

"That way nothing is accomplished, he thought. His mouth was too dry to speak but he could not reach for the water now. I must get him alongside this time, he thought. I am not good for many more turns. Yes you are, he told himself. You're good for ever" (pp. 101-02). And there are sentences and phrases where in its simplicity Hemingway's language has the prophetic tone of timeless truth: "Pain does not matter to a man." "I am glad we do not have to try to kill the stars." "Man is not much beside the great birds and beasts."

There are really only two characters in The Old Man and the Sea-- the old man and a boy. The rest of the figures who appear--the fishermen, the restaurant proprietor, and the tourists--are merely part of the setting of the Cuban fishing village.

3

The boy, Manolin, appears only at the beginning and end of the novel, but the old man thinks about him frequently: "I wish the boy was here." He is the only person who loves the old man. He brings him coffee and black beans and rice, helps him with his fishing gear, and would go fishing with him if his parents allowed him to.

The old man, Santiago, is a simple, uneducated fisherman, but his long years of struggle with the sea have given him wisdom, dignity, and integrity. Though he kills fish for his living, he feels a sense of kinship with them and with all other living creatures. He even talks to the fish and birds. Despite his age, he is still extremely strong; and his attempt to capture and bring home, single-handedly, a huge marlin, fails only because the sharks eat the marlin after he has finally caught it. At the end, with nothing to show for his three days and nights alone in a small boat except the skeleton of a huge fish, he returns to his shack, physically exhausted but with his spirit unbroken.

Santiago's defeat by a nature he loves but whose destructive potential he recognizes is clearly a symbol for the plight of man as Hemingway sees it. This plight Hemingway has seen in his earlier novels as well. Lieutenant Henry, at the end of A Farewell to Arms, says: "You never had time to learn. They threw you in and told you the rules and the first time they caught you off base they killed you . . . . They killed you in the end. You could count on that."[2] His heroes in The Sun Also Rises and For Whom the Bell Tolls learn the same lesson in the end. Hemingway's theme is the most clearly stated in The Old Man and the Sea, where it is removed from the confusions of war, politics, or love. Simply stated, this theme is the situation of man in his environment, against which he must struggle with all the strength, courage, and dignity at his command until it defeats him, as it inevitably will. As Carlos Baker says, "The tragic view of life comes out in his perennial contrast of the permanence of nature and the evanescence of man. Here also is something about the nature of manhood."[3]

There are other possible levels of interpretation of The Old Man and the Sea. Some critics have seen in the old man's fight with the sharks a symbolic representation of Hemingway and the hostile critics who attacked his previous novel, Across the River and Into the Trees. The old man's wounded hands and back, and his final staggering walk up the beach, carrying the mast on his back, may also be seen as Christian symbolism. The critic Joseph Waldmeir writes:

> In recent years, critics have become increasingly suspicious that it is necessary to read Ernest Hemingway's work on the symbolic as well as on the story level in order to gain a full appreciation of its art . . . . The Old Man and the Sea, while reasserting the set of values, the philosophy which permeates all of Hemingway, is built upon the great abstractions—love and truth and honor and loyalty and pride and humility—and again speaks of the proper method of attaining and retaining these virtues, and of the spiritual satisfaction inevitably bestowed upon their holder.[4]

The universality of these great abstractions is part of the appeal of this book. The reader feels sympathy for and pride in the old man, who can be regarded as a symbol of all mankind. In _The Old Man and the Sea_, Hemingway has written a fine novel which should appeal to many men in many places.

Footnotes

[1] Ernest Hemingway, The Old Man and the Sea (New York: Scribners, 1952).

[2] Ernest Hemingway, A Farewell to Arms (New York: Scribners, 1929), p. 338.

[3] Carlos Baker, Hemingway (Princeton: Princeton University Press, 1952), p. 298.

[4] Joseph Waldmeir, "Confiteor Hominem: Ernest Hemingway's Religion of Man," PMLA, 42 (1956), 277.

Bibliography

Baker, Carlos. <u>Hemingway</u>. Princeton: Princeton University Press, 1952.

Hemingway, Ernest. <u>A Farewell to Arms</u>. New York: Scribners, 1929.

_____. <u>The Old Man and the Sea</u>. New York: Scribners, 1952.

Waldmeir, Joseph. "Confiteor Hominem: Ernest Hemingway's Religion of Man." <u>PMLA</u>, 42 (1956), 277-81.

SAMPLE OUTLINE (STORY)

A Critical Review of Stephen Crane's

"The Open Boat"

I. The "new" prose of Stephen Crane

    A. Impact of Crane on contemporary writers

        1. Praised by Howells, Garland, Conrad

        2. Quotation: opening three sentences of story

    B. Qualities of Crane's prose

        1. Intimate details

        2. Vivid sense of color

        3. Strong sense of physical form

II. Structure of "The Open Boat"

    A. Point of view

        1. So-called "concealed narrator"

            a. Constantly changing

            b. Extremely close to characters

        2. Permits great fidelity to physical sensations

        3. Pattern of alternating panoramas and small scenes

    B. Suspense

        1. Narrative covering about twenty-four hours

        2. Interest in fate of characters sustained until the very end

        3. Climax reached when boat is swamped in surf

    C. Conclusion of story skillfully handled

        1. Death of oiler significant

        2. Survivors seen as "interpreters" of the sea

III.   The Meaning of "The Open Boat"

    A.   Autobiographical elements

        1.   Crane's attempted trip to Cuba in 1896

        2.   Actual sinking of "Commodore"

    B.   Universalizing of personal experience

        1.   Episodes transformed from mere incidents in author's life

        2.   Through them, man seen experiencing and comprehending the futility and lack of meaning in life and death

SAMPLE OUTLINE (POEM)

A Critical Review of William Butler Yeats'

"A Prayer for My Daughter"

I. Background of the poem

   A. Ireland in 1919

   B. Yeats' political and social views

   C. Prophetic tone

      1. Events since 1919

      2. Relationship of poetic truth to reality

II. Subject of the poem

   A. Setting

      1. Autobiographical elements

         a. Old tower

         b. Gregor's wood

      2. Storm

      3. Night

   B. Characters

      1. Father (poet)

      2. Infant daughter

   C. Nature of "prayer"

III. Significance of allusions in the poem

   A. Allusions

      1. Helen of Troy

      2. Aphrodite ("that great queen")

      3. Hephaestus ("bandy-legged smith")

      4. Horn of plenty

5. Paris ("a fool")

B. Significance of allusions

1. Comparison: Helen's unhappiness with daughter's hoped-for happiness

2. Classical (permanent) values applied to contemporary life

IV. Imagery of the poem

A. Dominant images

1. Wind

a. Quotation (lines 10-12, 55-56)

b. Connotations

B. Contrasting relationships of these images

1. Paradox of "murderous innocence"

2. Juxtaposition of beautiful with non-beautiful (Helen-Hephaestus, Helen-Paris)

3. Contrast of "custom and ceremony" with "innocence and beauty"

C. Ultimate development of contrast of self-assertion (bad) with self-realization (good)

V. Theme of the poem

A. Allusions and images combined to reveal meaning

B. Theme: true stability and happiness (tree) in an unstable world (wind) do not come from natural gifts (innocence, beauty) alone but rather from acquired discipline (custom, ceremony)

C. Final quotation (lines 77-80)

SAMPLE OUTLINE (PLAY)

A Critical Review of Thornton Wilder's

The Skin of Our Teeth

I.   The Play as fantasy

    A.   The purpose of fantasy

        1.   Objectivity--to see familiar subjects in a new light

        2.   Shock effect on audience

    B.   Elements which contribute to fantasy in The Skin of Our Teeth

        1.   Strange juxtaposition of events

        2.   Anachronisms

        3.   Freedom from usual theatrical conventions

II. Symbolism as it suggests meaning

    A.   The theme: human problems and values are essentially alike in all ages: man is always threatened and must rise to the occasion

    B.   Examples of symbols in play

        1.   The ring

        2.   Mr. Antrobus' name

        3.   The ice

    C.   Character and symbolism

        1.   Mr. Antrobus

            a.   Inventor

            b.   "Veteran of foreign wars," "scars front and back"

        2.   Mrs. Antrobus

        3.   Sabina

            a.   Various roles

            b.   Function: a sort of chorus

4.   Henry Antrobus

III.   The elements of comedy

A.   Breach of theatrical convention

B.   Humorous dialogue

C.   Comic situations

IV.   Through the comic to the serious

A.   Restatement of theme

B.   Playful treatment of serious theme effective

1.   Avoids sentimentality

2.   Avoids triteness

3.   Increases the irony which is in itself central to the theme